Grand Mutation

poems about death, the cosmos,
& grandiosity

a tiny collection

poems by

Karyn Peyton

Finishing Line Press
Georgetown, Kentucky

Grand Mutation

poems about death, the cosmos,
& grandiosity

a tiny collection

Copyright © 2022 by Karyn Peyton
ISBN 978-1-64662-705-9 First Edition
All rights reserved under International and Pan-American Copyright Conventions. No part of this book may be reproduced in any manner whatsoever without written permission from the publisher, except in the case of brief quotations embodied in critical articles and reviews.

ACKNOWLEDGMENTS

Dad ~ *Kissing Dynamite*

Publisher: Leah Huete de Maines
Editor: Christen Kincaid
Cover Art: Rare Book Division, The New York Public Library. "The great comet of 1881" The New York Public Library Digital Collections. 1881 - 1882. https://digitalcollections.nypl.org/items/510d47dd-e81a-a3d9-e040-e00a18064a99
Author Photo: Karyn Peyton
Cover Design: Elizabeth Maines McCleavy

Order online: www.finishinglinepress.com
also available on amazon.com

Author inquiries and mail orders:
Finishing Line Press
PO Box 1626
Georgetown, Kentucky 40324
USA

Table of Contents

Page 1 - "Dad"

Page 2 - "Ren"

Page 3 - "Astrology"

Page 4 - "Uncle's Funeral Song"

Page 5 - "Grandpa"

Page 6 - "Homeless"

Page 7 - "Grasp the Medium"

Page 8 - "Education"

Page 9 - "I Lost Touch with What I Loved"

Page 10 - "Mom"

Page 11 - "Chicago Funeral"

Page 12 - "Pet"

Page 13 - "Mom II"

Page 14 - "List"

Page 15 - "True Story"

Page 16 - "Old"

Dad

I told my 92-year-old landlady that
My heat was up too high and she kept me down there for an hour just talking to me
About life and death and aging
 and race and church
And human things lady across the alley
 with too many cats
Man upstairs who blares at his mother
 on national holidays like a forlorn
Foghorn Ooo he is noisy
 smoking on the landing she said
And he's always coming in here with his face all
 beat up
Like he's been with the wrong crowd
 if you know what I mean she giggled
She hugged me like a bear and I love you
 you bring me joy
I see you changing My baby
 My brother died recently she admitted
How she missed barbecues on the back porch
 six homes in this house
And nobody says hello or grills steaks
 anymore

Do generations regenerate
 does growing up grow you out of yourself
Does it take your passions and mature you
 and cure you
So you can write it for once by a black lamp
On a legal pad I miss you Dad

Ren

Oh, I was an early bird
An early bird
This morning

She made me an early bird
An early bird
In mourning

So young   came the shriek   so young
I clung   to her wings   as she   rose

Astrology

Just where in this celestial clock   do I feel safe?
Is it under a grey blanket   wrapped around the toes
Is it really in the dark
    filled with crooked things that make it hard
                                      to grow old
I keep looking there   I don't find much
                          except on Jupiter days
By the light of a meaner moon   it's blown out
                          and erased
How'd it come to you to fathom these times?

Uncle's Funeral Song

"Fields of Gold" is good for the drive
"Stairway to Heaven" is great but it's sad so
                              don't play it the whole time
We're cowboys but don't what's that word
                              parody   it
Pick a country song that doesn't have
                              'hell'   in it
Or beer   what was that one he liked
                 that's vague sister   you know the one
"Another One Bites the Dust"?   you're terrible
                      ask Weston   Zeb's son
Not that one   it's too sad
                            just sad—sad   oh

Put him in the ground   to that one

Grandpa

Grandpa you gotta get outta here
                                        I know the bed's comfy
But the chaplain I don't trust her   Mom called her
                                                                   a kook
Thinks you're going to heaven
                              I think you're gonna hang around
You gotta buy some   underwear
                         before the outlet   closes down

Homeless

The convenience of a Prius does not stop
At its unrivaled gas mileage
Its lighthearted taxi cab attaché
Its allegory
To Emma Stone   no, sir   it does not stop
It is also a pantry
Storage locker
Renegade against local law enforcement   for example
When you encounter a drunk driver pitstop on the edge of Beverly
Hills
Prius piled high with cockroach traps
Crackers
All sorts of other nonsense   and dare I say
You look rather suspicious
Caravanning into 90210
With a mobile   proletarian
Time capsule   God, the *homeless*!
Booms from a mansion   now, what spares you
Arbitrary arrest   by the ever-picayune   LAPD
Is the fact
That you are driving   the most innocuous
Hatchback   in Los Angeles
                nay, the country
                      perhaps the world.

Grasp the Medium

Rugged   off-road   public intellectual
                                                           America
Doesn't produce   often   enough

If Keats read   milk and honey
                                                  would it distract him
From his hatred   of Byron   or not?

Education

I spend so much time
                not even in this world
Overwork my head so much
                lose my call to arms
The sacred poets' physicality
                should not be forgot

I Lost Touch with What I Loved

When I was six   I heard orchestral noises
When I gritted my teeth   and I read dreams
On the backs of my eyelids   with a luminous paper
Lantern   and these moments I called epiphanies
But poorly-nursed   they receded
                                          into my ears
Into my drums   those second opinions
                                          marching along
I dearly sought but didn't need   And then at thirteen
                                          I observe
That my girl feet   won't always be
                                          attached to the floor
With strings   of will-be's   and right-here's
                                          and I scream
Is it almost gone?
This is it   green turns in the river   is this it?
Way out   past the porch now
     cavorting in a field   not of this life
Is a sludge   of compassionate resentment
                          that's drizzled   like
gasoline   Around this resting house
        out there   as I peel and burn

I hear cymbals crashing

Mom

The past five minutes some scientist's been blow-horning
On the TV about these   these   growths
We can grow buildings now
      as opposed to pouring or   assembling them

Like nature isn't our mother anymore

But they still can't make hearts
      beat somewhere they won't
Her neck craned   my way   her critic's index
      jangling
Can you imagine growin' a skyscraper
      like a   tomato plant
Shit   and so she pressed   back

Chicago Funeral

We'll have to take you up to Andersonville to dance
I was immature and insecure as she half-drove,
half-plowed through the snow
With her tangerine light
And her camcorder on her lap,
Effortless and not thinking about me
But smiling at me
Significantly

Had she known I was anchoring my love for her
In the winter weather

Would it have changed that terrible April
Had another winter been available
For dancing   or more?
In a hurry   what for?

Pet

Kitty sagged   and I wailed

It was her radical tactic to get me to be as loving
Until the day I dropped

Mom II

So all afternoon the back				neighbor
						has been playing that shit kickin'
Heel slappin'			country bullshit		makes me want
To send a			bomb			over there

List

Today I:

Took a meaningful shower.

Picked out songs for the service.

Went on a drive.

Has to be enough.

The inscrutable fact that it could mean nothing at all

Dashes my heart against the cement
Just dashes it to pieces.

True Story

Today I found out I have five siblings

Three older, two marines
One younger with special needs

In Jersey, Peoria, the ocean, Berlin
And I already have an identical twin

If 2020 didn't just blot my ink

Old

The Ferris wheel is too rusty now
Standing firm before dark cloud after dark cloud
I found joy in its inching blue carts
Like tassels on a Christmas cupcake or anything round
Propped up by kind, predictable forces
Like wind and the workday
When a hot dog sails between the bars
The sun traveling over my knees
The memory, it's scalding hot
These racing artifacts, were they a prophecy
But my true thoughts never spoke
They bubbled up like islands, and I knew
I would be tired and familiar with what's hard to surrender
Hard to surrender what you hadn't signed off
Now I surrender, I surrender
I watched Katrina hit in 2005 not knowing he would be gone three years later
I watched this disease sweep the nation not knowing a different poison would kill him in August
I watched her die in my arms not knowing the marriage bill was passing that morning
Does anyone else feel uncomfortable
With the sun traveling over our knees
Day after day
This illness, it poses us to ask, and I quote
Whether it will bear any meaningful relation to our life's work
And can therefore be retrieved as a tragic turn
Or whether it is merely a random and meaningless act of violence
Some sick and impossible thing
Perpetrated by a pernicious and impersonal force
Why, it reminds me of every death I've ever witnessed
I got the photos out of the shed
I took a long hard look at all of them
Now I understand
And I surrender
I surrender

Karyn is a poet and TV writer living and working in Los Angeles. She grew up in a family of car people and savvy bookkeepers in Arizona. A first-generation college student, she received the Odyssey Scholarship to study at the University of Chicago and Oxford University, wrote for an independent documentary series about police misconduct, implemented sustainability programs in Lithuania for the US Department of State's VSFS Program, and made a guerilla-style documentary that severed a university's relationship with a psychiatric hospital. Her co-director's sudden passing sent her from Chicago to Los Angeles. She's spoken openly about the suicide epidemic among young people as a convocation speaker, and she was recently selected to develop a pilot about hate speech and safe spaces in higher education for the Nostos Screenwriting Workshop.

When Karyn isn't writing, she teaches Shakespeare in Scottish prisons through the Prison Education Project. She is also the proud mom of a rotund black cat.

Poetry first emerged as her passion when she was struggling with brevity in her writing. Now she gets straight to the point.